Cuba Travel Gui

PUBLISHED BY: (Steve R)

TABLE OF CONTENTS

Contents

Introduction

Cuba vacations are leading the way in travel to the Caribbean and for many good reasons. It is very affordable, it has excellent tourism infrastructure, it is a very safe destination and most of all it suits the needs and styles of all types of travel. Being the largest island in the Caribbean, Cuba boasts an array of terrain from spectacular pristine beaches to mountainous rainforests which make this communist nation a true getaway for any vacation. Eco-tourists, beach lovers, nature and culture fanatics all flock to Cuba in droves to discover the splendor of the island. If you are thinking of discovering this magnificent destination for the first time, here is a breakdown of the most popular resort areas and what you can expect at each.

=

Varadero for families, beach lovers, water sports

The most popular resort area in Cuba, Varadero is world-famous for the spectacular beaches and all-inclusive resorts. Miles of sugar white sand and warm, calm, turquoise waters greet thousands of sun worshippers annually looking for a relaxing holiday. The all-inclusive resorts that line the beaches are your source of hours of activities both on land and in the water and also provide accommodation for all budgets from modest to luxury.

The Cayos for couples, beach lovers, divers

On the north coast is a group of islands and inlets known as the Cayos. Cayo Coco, Cayo Guillermo and Cayo Santa Maria are just a few of these relatively isolated resort locations. Much like Varadero, the Cayos also have pristine beaches but the offshore reefs also provide some of the best diving in the Caribbean. As a quieter location, the Cayos are popular with honeymooners and couples looking for a romantic getaway.

Holguin for eco tourists, divers, beach lovers

Also on the north coast, Holguin is a nice blend of everything Cuba has to offer with great beaches, excellent diving, and the city has a nice blend of history, culture and architecture. Accommodation in the area is mostly all-inclusive resorts and mainly range around good 3 or 4 star resorts. Holguin is a good destination for a first timer to Cuba that wants a taste of everything on a smaller scale.

Santiago de Cuba for eco tourists, culture, history, diving

The beaches are not the top draw in Santiago de Cuba but the reefs and outlying areas attract divers to the depths in search of adventure. Outside of the resort area, the Sierra Maestra Mountains are perfect for eco-tourists, nature lovers and hikers with incredible flora and fauna, zip lining and safari tours through the rainforests. Most resorts in the area are all-inclusive and hover around an average rating.

Cienfuegos for singles, culture, history, diving

The town of Trinidad is a UNESCO world heritage site and is the best example of Spanish colonial architecture in the Caribbean. Accommodation tends to be more on the modest side and the beaches although not as stunning as on the northern coast, are still better than average and offer amazing snorkeling and diving. Not the first place I would recommend as a first timer to Cuba, it is definitely worth a visit through the scenic and visually appealing buildings of the old city.

Havana for history, culture

Once one of the richest cities in the Americas, Havana's decorated past is full of both triumph and misfortune. From the days of pirates sacking the city, and up to the revolution led by Fidel Castro and Che Guevara, Havana has accumulated centuries worth of stories and legends all of which have added to the history and culture of this capital city. Although no real beaches, a trip to Havana is full of life and insight. Museums and landmarks are scattered throughout and tell about the past and present of Cuba. Hotels in Havana range from apartment style bungalows to first class hotels and veer away from resort style options.

Cuba is a country of dynamic culture that features amazing beaches and an incredible range of travel options. It is a destination in which anyone can come away from feeling fulfilled and satisfied providing you choose the right area for your travel style.

TRAVELING TO CUBA FOR THE FIRST TIME? EVERYTHING YOU NEED TO KNOW!

Cuba is a history-rich destination which, like all travels, will open your eyes and view of the world like probably never before. You will find that the rumors you have heard about this destination are true. It does feel like time in Cuba stopped in early 1959 when Fidel's revolution succeeded and Batista had to flee the country. Here are the things you need to know if you are traveling to Cuba for the first time and are planning to explore farther than the all-inclusive hotels.

Traveling to Cuba for the First Time

There are two currencies The peso CUP and the convertible peso CUC. The CUP is the national currency, in Spanish moneda nacional. The CUC, paired with the US dollar, is mainly the "tourist" currency. Currently, 1 CUC is 25 CUP. Before going there, I thought locals couldn't access the CUC and vice versa. However, I saw many locals handling CUC and I was able to change CUC to CUP on a currency exchange office, which was useless as essentially almost everything is listed with both prices on tourist areas, but I did get a 3 pesos Che Guevara note which I wanted.

Takeaway: don't try to get CUP, and don't confuse the currencies when being given change. Here is a picture of both for reference, as you can see CUCs say "pesos convertibles". The best place to exchange money is the bank, not an exchange office and beware, if you take USD to exchange you will be charged a 10% fee so try to exchange any other currency.

"Casas Particulares" are the Cuba's Airbnb and a gem!

Since 1997, long before Airbnb existed, the government has allowed Cuban homeowners to rent rooms in their house for a fee. Houses have typically 2-3 rooms and the price ranges from 20-50 USD or CUC, sometimes including breakfast. Now that Cuba made peace with the US, you might be able to book a casa via Airbnb. Otherwise use TripAdvisor, it does not disappoint. As casas can't accommodate many guests, they sell out in advance so book with time either emailing or calling the casa which is the preferred option.

In my opinion, a casa is the best way to experience Cuba. If you pick one with good reviews, the hosts will be most surely be lovely. This will give you the opportunity to interact with locals and have a chat about the Cuban way of life. I was lucky to stay in this lovely casa in Santiago de Cuba where three generations of the family were present during my visit. The difference of opinions depending on the generation was mind blowing. Talking to them, definitely one of the highlights of the trip. Just to put it into perspective, I'm still in touch with the casa owners.

You wouldn't imagine the things casa owners have done to make our stay better. From gifting us a rum just because, to taking us to the hospital and convincing the doctor to not take us to another city in an ambulance and buying medicine for us so it would be 10 times cheaper!

Getting internet is a costly feat, so plan in advance

Forget about free Wi-Fi wherever you go, and say hello to internet cafes like back in the day! Internet is severely restricted and internet access controlled by the government. In a 5 star hotel I've had to purchase a small piece of paper with a code to get Wi-Fi access for 5 CUC an hour. In smaller towns, I have had to go to internet cafes where I had to pay a high price for timed usage. And yes, most of the times I'd have to queue, as Cubans also want to get on the internet.

It's similarly expensive for telephone calls. So if you are going to make calls from one of your casas make sure you pay them. This is part of the reason why a Cuban holiday is good, you really do disconnect! Make sure you download the maps you need on Google Maps and print any other documents you might need to show.

Cubans have their own way of queuing

This is important, you'll avoid potential arguments with Cubans/annoyance with yourself for being ignorant. Cubans don't queue on a straight line. They arrive to the queue, and ask "Quien es el último?" or just "el último?". Someone will say "yo" and you know that's the person who goes before you. You are essentially asking who is the last person in the queue. If you don't do this, you are not considered as being in the queue. This is for real. Always ask for "el ultimo".

There is no crime. Well, depends on how you define crime...

Cuba is a communist country, and therefore capitalism is almost null. This means no advertising other than propaganda and no consumerism. This results in almost all Cubans not being able to access most of the items we use on a day-to-day and on our trips, like a GoPro, Nike shoes and other really basic stuff you wouldn't believe. As an example, it took me ages to find somewhere that sold a lighter. However, unless you are very unlucky it's unlikely that you would get mugged. As always, take care of your belongings, but Cuba is safe enough for you to fully relax.

However, I did notice some cheeky innocent crimes. For instance, in the famous restaurant "La Bodeguita Del Medio" I was overcharged in various items in my bill, by small amounts like 1 CUC or 0.5 CUCs per item, twice – and I went twice! This happened in other restaurants as well (the bill is handwritten most of the times). Other similar things happened and, in all cases, the people involved almost didn't apologize which kind of led me to believe it wasn't really a mistake. Just keep your eyes open, sometimes you may let it go and consider it "extra tip" for how friendly they are, but let it be your choice. Also, get away from people talking to you on the streets specially in Havana. Although they look like they want to be your friends and are super nice, I'm afraid it's probably a scam.

Food can be a little bit meh

As said before, buying options in Cuba are limited as it's a closed country. You'll be amazed to see in supermarkets how there is only one (or two) options of each item. And, if you check the labels, you'll realize they belong to local companies which are government owned.

Similarly, there are not many food options: the fruits you'll get will be the ones in season. There will be a lot of "moros con cristianos" (rice with beans) with pork, chicken or fish, sometimes with plantains or sweet potatoes. Beef is scarce, and even in 5 stars hotel I'd suggest you avoid it, you'll be at risk of intoxication (it happened to my travel companion, and it wasn't fun). And last, milk is mostly available in its powder form as fresh milk is very scarce. The best food you'll get will be at the Paladares, which are privately owned restaurants. These, compared to their government owned counterparts, need to make a bigger effort to survive so they are generally much better quality.

Visiting Cuba - Tips on Planning Your Holiday Or Vacation

While I always think Planning a Holiday is as much fun as the holiday itself. Cuba may be more of a challenge, than usual, if you are planning an independent itinerary.Planning your holiday or vacation in this fascinating country could well become an exercise in compromise and decision making , as you decide what you will do and what you must leave out.

Finding out the information you need is not always easy for Cuba, especially if you are planning your holiday independently. The criteria for visas and best currency to take, does change. Do not reply on an old Lonely Planet. The questions below are important - be sure to answer each, and then decide the best travel plan for you.

- How do you get there?

- Where should you stay?

- How can you best get around ?

- What currency should you take ?

- Do you need a visa?

- Do you need to worry about the weather?

- Is Cuba a safe country for travelling?

- What sort of food will they have?

All these questions may seem daunting, when you review the options.But they are overcome by working through them one by one. Cuba is a little different to other countries, with more restrictions and limitations.It does depend on which country you are from, what the criteria for visas, and travel to Cuba will be. e.g.Getting there is not as simple as just getting on a plane, as you cannot fly directly from USA.

Firstly decide how long you will be in the country. You will almost certainly have nowhere near enough time to fit everything on your list into the time frame you have for your holiday. So decide what is most important to you.

Cuba is not a cheap destination! Take a reasonable amount of cash.Credit cards are limited in use to large hotels.Be sure you check your card will be accepted . They do not take many credit cards. The cost of each transaction is also very expensive, so cards are best used only for large amounts.

Cuba may be a relatively small country, but their variety of geographic areas, gives you many choices in activities and places to visit. Historic towns, beautiful beaches and interesting sights mean you will find your activities and attractions list will offer a vast selection of both outdoor excitement, wonderful music and indoor culture.

Here are some tips for planning your Cuban itinerary:

- Accommodation - Hotels or Casa Particulares - You will need to decide what level of comfort you require! A Casa is a good way to see Cubans in their own homes.

- Negotiation - If you are travelling with another person, or your family, the art of compromise will no doubt have to come into play. Each choose several activities you want to do, and then negotiate if time means some cannot be included! The beach at Varadero or the historic town of Trinidad - they re very different places to spend your time.

- Travelling Solo - Deciding how you travel will be a little easier if you travel on your own. Although you will still be limited to what you have time for, and what suits your budget. Travelling solo will perhaps send you in a different direction. Maybe a tour, or semi independent tour will work best. Or are you just going to take local transport or share a rental car or taxi with others you meet along the way.

- Package Deals - Some activities are fun, but expensive. Look out for package deals if you want to go to a resort. You can get "all inclusive deals ", for often quite a considerable saving.

- Independent Travel or a Tour - A tour might work better for you, rather than travelling independently. Perhaps a bicycle tour, or Intrepid tour where you still have plenty of independent time. stay in a mix of hotels and Casa's so have the best of both worlds.For some of you the full hotel tour will be your chosen option.

- Culture or Beaches -Do you want to see the historic and cultural Cuba, or are you going for the beach, sun and sand?

- Getting Around - Will it be by bus, mini bus, taxi - perhaps shared, rental car or bicycle.

Ensure you allow enough travelling time between places. Travel in Cuba is slower than you might expect, with limited transport options, and connections that may not always be timed for a smooth transition. E.g. Buses from Vinales get to Havana too late to connect the same day for Trinidad.

If you decide to hire a car, the distances invariably take longer than they look on a map. So do use a distance calculator, and check the road conditions. Travel could be slow on the less than perfect roads!

Cuba Opens The Emigration Pressure Valve Again

After 51 years of keeping its people virtual prisoners on their island, Cuba is tearing down the biggest barrier: its exit visa requirement. The next question is where, exactly, will Cubans be welcome when they go?

Beginning Jan 1st 2017 most Cubans will be permitted to travel with only a passport and an entry visa from the countries they intend to visit. Cuban travelers will also be allowed to stay abroad for 24 months (up from 11 months) without losing their Cuban residency or health care coverage.

There are significant exceptions to the new rule. The government will continue to restrict travel to protect national security and "human capital." The national security exception will probably apply to military personnel, and perhaps to dissidents or to senior government officials and their relatives. The second exception will prevent certain professionals, including doctors and scientists, from taking their skills elsewhere. This is particularly important for Cuba, because it uses its doctors' services to barter with oil-rich Venezuela. As of last year, around 40,000 Cuban doctors and other professionals were stationed in Venezuela in exchange for around 115,000 barrels of oil a day.

Those who are permitted to leave will face other obstacles. The cost of a Cuban passport is expected to double to $100 - about five times the country's average monthly salary - as the new policy takes effect. Cuban travelers will also need to find a way to pay for transportation off the island. Currently, round-trip airfare between Havana and Miami on an established charter runs around $400.

But there are good reasons to believe that the Castro regime, now headed by President Raul Castro, brother of Fidel Castro, genuinely wants to make it easier for Cubans to leave. These reasons have little to do with any newfound interest in personal freedom and plenty to do with self-interest.

Remittances - money sent from outside the country, usually by relatives - are an important source of hard currency on the island. Last year remittances totaled an estimated $2.3 billion. To put this figure in perspective, Cuba's gross domestic product is only about $60 billion. Allowing more Cubans to leave would create more foreign wage-earners who would be likely to send part of their paychecks back to family members left behind. The extended travel period included in the new policy may also allow Cubans who do not wish to leave permanently to spend time abroad earning money that they would then bring back to Cuba.

The regime's goals are probably not solely economic, however. As pressure for change continues to build, the move may serve as a way for the Castros to quickly get rid of those who are most dissatisfied. As Raul Hernandes-Morales, a Cuban-American lawyer in Miami who left Cuba at the age of 15, told The New York Times, "Every once in a while they open up the pressure cooker and let out some steam." (1)

The last time the pressure valve opened was in the spring of 1980, during the Mariel boatlift. The effect was, predictably, explosive. The pressure had built to an extreme high; in the midst of economic distress, Cubans had flooded the Peruvian embassy seeking asylum. Ultimately, the Cuban government opened the port of Mariel to those wishing to leave the country, so long as they could arrange their own transportation. Cuban-Americans in Florida responded by heading south in large numbers, in pretty much anything they could find that would float, to help provide that transportation. The U.S. government agreed to accept the refugees, but not to transport them.

The mass exodus led to overcrowding on boats, producing unsafe conditions that killed 27 people. U.S. immigration officials were overwhelmed by the influx. They soon discovered that some of the refugees were criminals and mental patients who had been put on boats directly after being released from prisons and institutions. As officials tried to screen the new arrivals, the approximately 125,000 "Marielitos" were held for processing in refugee camps that were as overcrowded as the boats the refugees had travelled on. At Fort Chaffee Army Reserve base in Arkansas, the conditions were so bad that refugees rioted, and 40 were injured in clashes with federal marshals.

To prevent the problems of the Mariel boatlift from recurring, we will need to reconsider our approach to Cuban immigration. Since 1995, the United States has maintained what is known informally as the "wet foot, dry foot" policy, under which those who are intercepted while trying to reach the States are turned back, but those who successfully reach U.S. soil are permitted to stay and are automatically given the option of embarking on the path to citizenship after one year. Our current policy, combined with Cuba's new opening, could lead Cubans seeking to settle in the United States to first leave Cuba by obtaining entry visas to other countries, and then later trying to cross the U.S.border illegally. It is easy to see how this would create chaos, not to mention rampant unfairness, along the U.S.-Mexican border, as Cubans who slip across are permitted to stay while Mexicans and others are sent back. The Cubans will accordingly be targets for all sorts of abuse in Mexico as well.

One possible response would be for the U.S. to adopt less permissive policies toward Cuban immigrants once they can, theoretically, emigrate legally to any place willing to admit them. The far better option, however, would be to use this opportunity to allow Cuban immigrants who leave Cuba legally to enter the U.S. in the same way (and to overhaul and liberalize our other immigration policies, as well). The best cure for illegal immigration is legal immigration.

CUBA: BARACOA AND ITS SURROUNDINGS

The place where the City of Baracoa is today, was first visited by Admiral Christopher Columbus on November 27th, 1492. There was a village there, and the Spanish decided to found the first city or village in 1511. That is the reason why it is known as Ciudad Primada (the first city). It is said that its name is a word of aruaco origin meaning "existence of the sea". Other places of the Cuban geography have similar roots and always related with the water, as for instance, Guanabacoa, Guasabacoa, Jibacoa and others.

Baracoa is also called the City of Rains (it rains almost all the year) and the City of the Landscapes or Paradise City because of the beauty of its surroundings. The mountains surround the city, specially one tableland, quoted by Admiral Christopher Columbus in his navigation Diary in 1492. This tableland can be seen from almost every near spot, so sailors used it as a reference to navigate in the area until the Punta de Maisí lighthouse was built.

This elevation is known as El Yunque de Baracoa (Baracoa Anvil) and is the emblem of the city. It has almost vertical slopes and flat top. Some travelers compare this mountain with the Bluefountain tableland in South Africa.

Large transparent rivers flow into the bays of Baracoa and Miel, as well as the Toa, the Duaba, Miel and Macaguanigua rivers flow into the Playuelas, Toa and Duaba beaches. The natural vegetation in the near elevations is made of virgin forests of great beauty, being outstanding the pine forests, while along the rivers, there is a line of trees that follow the river course known as gallery forests.

Thanks to the humid tropical climate, there is a great variety of fruit in the area, while in the coast, the river mouths and the near places the coconut and almond trees grow, which gives the place a touch of paradise. The green and the blue are the predominating colors in these places.

This region is considered to have one of the largest reserves of wood, cocoa and coconut in Cuba. The recipes elaborated with these last two products and its derivates are unique in Cuba. Ask for the "Cucurucho" and you will know. Its content and flavor are marvelous, while its presentation is very typical. We recommend tasting it.

After booking in one of the Baracoa hotels, you will think of what to do. The city has everything to enjoy its beauties because it has the appropriate infrastructure. You can think of visiting natural places as beautiful as the National Park Alejandro de Humboldt, the city and its surroundings. We will give you a brief description of the city for we expect the details to be discovered by yourself.

If you look in your map, you will see that Baracoa is a city that has grew embraced to the sea, at the Eastern of the bay of the same name. It is not very big and has a central part and to the South the Paradise neighborhood. A seawall borders the entire coast to the open sea. Baracoa was named the capital of Cuba in 1518 until 1521 when the capital was transferred to Santiago de Cuba. It had a first shield, which was forgotten in time and replaced for the current one that dates from 1833. It was almost isolated from the rest of Cuba until 1965. That is why it preserves many of its old traditions.

Being a coastal city, as Havana, Guanabacoa and other Cuban cities, Baracoa suffered the siege and attacks of pirates during part of the 18th century. That is why the governors built fortresses to set the artillery for the defense, which are still preserved, being places of great historical interest. One of them is located at Bahia de Miel (Honey Bay) that is Morrillo Chico o Majana fortress; while the other three are in the city. Those are La Punta (today is a restaurant), Seboruco or Santa Bárbara or La Villa (today a hotel), and the Matachín, which today is the

Municipal Museum of Baracoa, opened as such in 1981. There you can see things of the native´s culture, historical objects, natural science specimen and numismatic and philatelic collections.

Nuestra Señora de la Asunción Parish is a relic of the city from the historical and cultural point of view. It is one of the first churches built in the first years of the 16th century when the village was founded. Inside of it there is the Parra Cross, the only one preserved of the 29 crosses that it is said the Admiral placed in America.

In Baracoa, the Ecotur Travel Agency offers different options to visit the mountains or other places of interest such as El Yunque Path (the Anvil Path), the visit to the Archeology Museum Cueva del Paraíso (Paradise Cave), navigation along the To a river, the largest in Cuba and a tour to Duaba Property. Next we give you a brief description of these tours, which we recommend to make.

El Yunque Path has about 8 km of length. It is made on foot and the grade of difficulty to make it is medium. An advantage to do it is that the large Duaba River flows next to the base of this elevation, which influences the nice and fresh microclimate of the place. The tableland is of limestone rock and to climb it is very much like the classical mogotes (flat topped hillocks), where the vegetation is similar although there are ferns and other representatives of the humidity.

Birds can be seen and heard such as some woodpecker species, the Tocororo (Priotelus temnurus), the Zunzún (Mellisuga helenae) and others. Also one can see the jutías (Capromys sp.), reptiles and butterflies of different species, all of them of great beauty.

40 Things You Must Know Before Traveling To Cuba (Especially If You're American)

Cuba has always been a bucket-list country for many travelers, but since the recent reestablishment of diplomatic conversations between the U.S. and Cuba, the country rose to the spotlight to become a prime destination for American travelers. In the last year alone, tourism in Cuba boomed exponentially. Not only more travelers from around the world are visiting it, but now Americans added themselves to the tourism mix, even when they are still not quite in the "I can visit Cuba green zone."

Getting There and Some Planning

1. Most People Need A Visa

Travelers from 19 countries can travel to Cuba without a visa. Travelers from the rest of the world can purchase a "Tourist Card" at the airport before checking into their flight. Americans, it's a bit more complicated. To this date, only Americans traveling under these 12 visa categories are allowed to travel to Cuba, including family visits, official visits, journalistic, professional, educational and religious activities, and public performances. These visas can be obtained via a tour company or the Cuban Embassy in Washington DC. Regular tourism is still forbidden. But, don't worry, there's still a way to travel there as a regular tourist, and hopefully, in the future, it will be much easier as diplomatic talks lift most of the current restrictions.

2. Cuba WILL welcome you even if you're an American without an "Approved Visa" from the U.S.

While the U.S. still has "issues" allowing everyone to travel to Cuba freely, Cuba, on the other hand, does welcome everyone to their country, as long as they have a valid "Tourist Card"

3. There are direct flights from the US, but...

Anyone not from the U.S. can simply fly from their country. Easy. Americans with a visa can fly from one of the 10 (current) cities with direct flights to Cuba via a Special Authority Charter.

Update: Flying direct from the US is now easier than before and available to almost anyone (from select cities). According to Curious Nomad, an American who visited Cuba on December 2016 (flying with Spirit Airlines direct to Havana), you can now buy the Tourist Card at the airport for $100 if flying with Spirit Airlines and Southwest Airlines (which is five times the amount you'll pay in Mexico, for example. See Point #4). Apparently, for all other airlines, you still need to get a proper visa in one of the 12 categories.

Since this information might change at any moment, I'd recommend checking directly at the dedicated "Cuban travel" page of your airline to see if they sell the Tourist Card during check-in at the airport, for how much, and what documents are needed.

Alaska Airlines (They refer to third-party service)

American Airlines (They refer to third-party service)

Delta ($50 during check-in)

Frontier Airlines (No information at the moment. NOTE: Frontier's service to Cuba is set to end in early-June 2017)

JetBlue ($50 during check-in)

Southwest Airlines (They refer to third-party service at the airport)

Spirit Airlines (They refer to third-party service at the airport. NOTE: Spirit's service to Cuba is set to end in late-May 2017)

United ($50 during check-in)

4. The Stopover Technique is still an easy way to go, for regular American tourists.

Anyone from the U.S. wanting to visit as a regular tourist can do so by flying to a stopover country (like Mexico) and then flying from Mexico to Cuba. This "trampoline" technique has been used for decades by "rogue" American travelers. Mexico, Panama, Dominican Republic and the Bahamas are among the most popular stopover countries – though Mexico is almost always the cheapest.

An important detail here is that you must pass through immigration in this stopover country to be able to buy your "Cuban Tourist Card" during your flight check-in process there. At the moment (2015), the tourist card costs $20.

Another important detail would be to buy your flights as two different round trips. For example, Denver to Cancun as one round-trip, and Cancun to Havana as a separate round-trip.

5. You can enter with a US passport

The American passport presents no issue when entering Cuba, even without one of the 12 visas. Like I said, Cuba has no problem with American. Just buy your Tourist Card at your stopover country (or now even in the US) and once at Cuban immigration, they will only stamp your Tourist Card, not your passport. For non-visa holders, this will avoid some potential problem when returning to the US. I didn't have any issues when I returned to the US.

Update: Several American friends have gone to Cuba with an American passport and with only a tourist card bought at the airport and none of them had any issue coming back to the US. They actually said the US immigration agents didn't even bother asking further questions after they told them they just returned from Cuba.

6. Some search engines don't show flights to Cuba

Expedia, Orbitz, and other search engines don't show flights to Cuba. Period. At the time of writing, skyscanner.com, momondo.com, and kayak.com do show flights from the U.S. that can be purchased online. They show flights departing from the U.S. (and all over the world), but will warn you that you can only buy them if you have a visa – otherwise you will be denied boarding. You're not required to show proof of a visa when buying the airfare.

You can buy your flights and have no problem boarding after you buy the Tourist Card at the airport or the Embassy.

7. Best time to go there

Mid-November to March is the coolest, driest, and busiest season. May and June are the wet seasons, but Cuban highlights like the tobacco harvesting and carnival happen at this time. July to November is hurricane season, so there's a chance to stormy weather between these months – especially more towards late August to early October when it's the peak of the hurricane season.

8. Buy a tour or not?

If you want to take the easy, yet more expensive road, buy your tours before arriving in Cuba. Traveling Cuba is a hassle, but not impossibly hard if you're open to dealing with the struggles. In this case, don't buy your tours and wait until you get to Cuba. There, local agencies often offer tours and hotels for a fraction of the price (or the "national rates"). This is how I managed to stay in the

Melia Cayo Coco for about 1/3 of what it costs online. But, prepare to have a hard time finding tour shops in some cities. Also, your host can always recommend doing some tours, which often are run by locals, and not tour companies – adding to the local experience.

9. Print out your documents before leaving

Technology is not easily found in Cuba and while there I didn't see a single internet café. Print and take any travel documents, reservations, insurance, or other information you need before leaving.

10. You need travel insurance

It is required to have travel insurance to enter Cuba. They may or may not ask for proof at the airport, and should you not have any, they could deny your entry. I wasn't asked, nor other people I've asked or read about their entry to Cuba.

Money

11. Americans can't use debit or credit cards

And this sucks. As of September 2015, the Cuban Sanctions imposed by the U.S. does not allow any American to withdraw money or pay with a debit or credit card while in Cuba. In fact, I got my bank account frozen just for signing up to my mobile banking while in Cuba. My bank didn't even want to unfreeze it until after I left the country and showed proof of it via a copy of my boarding pass. This restriction is supposed to be lifted soon as relationships improve, so I recommend checking for the latest updates regarding the sanctions on this page.

Other nationalities can use credit cards, where accepted.

Update: As of April 2017, American credit and debit cards seem to still not work in Cuba.

12. Tell your bank you're going to Cuba

While this is highly recommended every time you travel outside your country, when going to Cuba is is quite important (no matter which nationality). You will want to make sure your debit/credit card will work there.

13. It's all about taking lots of cash

Cuba is still mostly a cash economy, so even if you're not American, you should take enough money with you to last most of your trip. Americans, of course, have to take all their money cash.

Some companies are starting to accept credit cards and ATMs do allow withdrawals with non-American cards.

14. Don't take U.S. Dollars to exchange

Currency exchanges places are known as CADECAs. It is possible to exchange U.S. Dollars, Euros, British Pounds, Mexican Pesos, and a few other currencies, but the worst currency to exchange there is the U.S. Dollar. It gets charged a 10% fee in addition to the current exchange rate while all the other currencies don't get any additional fee.

Preferably, get Euros or British Pounds from the U.S., as these get the best exchange rates since they are more liquid. Or, withdraw money from an ATM at your stopover country in their local currency (preferably Mexico), to then exchange that in Cuba for Convertible Cuban Pesos.

15. Cuba has two currencies

This will be confusing at first, but you'll get used to it quickly. There are two currencies in Cuba: The National Peso (CUP), and the Convertible Peso (CUC). Funny enough, Convertible Pesos are valued at 1 to 1 with the U.S. Dollar, while the National Peso stands at about 26 pesos per dollar.

The money you should exchange for is the CUC, Convertible Peso, as this is the currency used for almost everything there (especially among tourists). I don't recommend exchanging for CUP since you're probably not going to use it at all. The CUP is only used for local transportation, to buy fruits and vegetables on the street, and some restaurants that cater more to locals. Should you need to use the public bus, for example, you can pay in CUC and get the change in CUP.

16. Always confirm which is the demanded currency

Whether it is CUC or CUP, Cubans simply call it "pesos". So, when someone says this is "2 pesos," you should make sure which one he is referring to as the amount is substantially different. You can ask, "is this in CUC or Moneda Nacional?" Or, if the price seems to be really high, them most probably it is in CUP.

Accommodation

17. The most common form of accommodation is known as Casa Particular

There are several hotels in Cuba, but the most common form of accommodation are the Casas Particulares. These are rooms or apartments rented by locals for a daily fee. Sometimes, you might rent an apartment for yourself while in other cases you might rent a room in a family's house and share the common spaces with them. Many families have turned their houses into Casas Particulares with several rooms to make a living in Cuba. If you can, stay in a Casa Particular for the local experience and to help the family's local business. The base price per night in a Casa Particular is $25+, which is a fraction of what you'll pay at a hotel.

18. Couchsurfing is "illegal"

While the site is not illegal itself, the act of staying at someone's place for free is illegal in Cuba. Under Cuban law, every foreigner must pay for accommodation unless they are friends with a local. In this case, the local must go to the appropriate agency with email exchanges, pictures, and other communications proving you know each-other. The authorities may or may not approve it.

19. Bookings are mostly through word of mouth

Given that the internet is still not widely accessible there, most hotels and casas particulares don't have internet, nor a website. Most bookings are done through the phone and recommendations from other locals. For example, I "couchsurfed" in Havana and my host from Havana recommended (and booked by phone) the other casas particulares where I stayed in Trinidad and Viñales.

Many Casas Particulares are using Airbnb to promote themselves without the need of a website. You should consider this option (and with this link you get $40 off your first booking). Or, Couchsurfing is another good option (though unlike the rest of the world, you still have to pay).

It is recommended to have at least the first night booked before arriving in Cuba. The rest you can book or extend as you go.

Update: Now sites like HotelsCombined are listing a mix of hotels and casas particulates you can reserve online.

Eating

20. Food in Cuba is nothing to brag about

Due to its trade restrictions, Cuba lacks in its culinary delights; so don't expect delicious meals. Yes, you can find good food here and there, but this is not the norm.

21. Don't drink the water

Simple and easy. Buy bottled water. Otherwise, your tummy and booty will not be happy about it.

22. Try eating only at Paladares Particulares.

Cuba has two types of restaurants, the state-run restaurants and the privately run ones known as paladares particulares. Try eating at the paladares particulares since they cost about the same as the state-run ones, but usually have better quality. As locals say, state-run restaurants don't care about the food quality since, in the end, they don't need the profits (because they are supported by the government). The private ones, on the other hand, if they are not good, they go bankrupt.

How to know which is state-run and which is private? Either ask them before ordering or just pay attention to where locals are eating and queuing. Cubans (who can afford to eat outside) don't like the state-run restaurants, so they prefer to queue at a paladar particular.

23. Don't eat from the really cheap local restaurants

I usually eat street food, from very cheap places, but Cuba was an exception. It is common to see places selling pizza and ice cream or other meals for a fraction of what they should cost and charged in CUP (like 10 CUP or $0.50 and much less). These foods, while cheap, are considered "garbage" by locals since they are done with local products of the lowest quality possible.

24. Take your favorite snacks with you

Not surprisingly, markets there don't offer much variety since they focus on selling items of first need to locals – which don't include sweets and snacks. You may find a few snacks here and there, but those are rare, and there will not be a lot of varieties.

Transportation

25. Cuba is relatively well connected by bus

You will be able to visit all major cities and travel all around the country by bus. While there are a few bus companies there, as far as I know, only Viazul is the one that takes tourists traveling independently.

26. Go to the bus station at least an hour before departure

While Viazul has a site with a current service schedule, it is not possible to book tickets online. You must go to the bus station ahead of time and queue for a ticket. Since buses are not that frequent, they tend to sell out quick. But, there's an option...

27. Shared taxis are also a good option

Taxi drivers stand in front of the bus station to pick the excess of passengers without tickets. They offer a shared taxi ride to some of the most popular and well-connected cities in Cuba for about the same price of the bus and faster. If you're going to a smaller town not covered by the shared taxi, you can take the shared taxi to the closest city possible, and from there take a local shared taxi called "Almendrones."

Should they price the shared taxi ride much higher than the bus, then, you'll need to haggle. Oh, and don't be surprised if the local sharing your ride paid a fraction of what you paid. That's Cuba. Foreigners almost always have to pay more than locals.

28. The local busses in Havana are fine, and so are the taxis.

Local buses cost 1 CUP (about $0.04 – which you can pay in CUP or give 5 cents of a CUC). It is hard to understand the routes, but your host could tell you which one's you should take to go to most of the important places. Taxis are not expensive, costing about 5 CUC from Old to Central Havana.

29. Vintage taxis have a set route

All those pretty vintage taxis you see in pictures, those are exclusive for tourists to ride (not drive) and they only go through a select route in Havana. You could, though, have the luck of riding a vintage car as your shared taxi from once city to the other.

30. Havana is walkable

Havana is big, but if you have a few days there, you can save money on transportation by walking it and seeing things at a slower pace. I do recommend walking; that's when you see the best scenes of the city. Prepare to sweat... I mean, sweat crazily!

Also, Viñales, Trinidad, and other popular cities can be walked easily.

Technology

31. Internet... don't count on it

Don't expect internet at your hotel or casa particular, and even if they have it, it will not be available for you to use it. Recently, the local telecommunications company (ETECSA) started adding WiFi hot spots on major cities, which can be used with the purchase of a WiFi card that allows you to use it for an hour.

Hot spots are found in select parks in Havana and in front of the ETECSA building in other cities. The cards can be bought at ETECSA and cost 2.50 CUC for an hour's use. They often run out of cards quickly due to the demand, so make sure to buy a few when available.

Oh, and don't expect the WiFi to be reliable or fast.

32. Get a Tarjeta Propia

A Tarjeta Propia is a phone card you can buy at ETECSA to make local phone calls in Cuba from any public phone – found all around the city in all cities. This was a saver for me when I needed to coordinate my arrival time with my hosts.

33. Don't expect roaming phone service

Simple… just don't count on it. Any (expensive) international call will have to be made from a phone center.

34. Use offline maps or preload your Google Maps

Galileo Offline Maps allows you to use your phone's GPS to show your location on regular and pre-uploaded maps from other sites (continued in next point). Of course, you'll download these before going to Cuba. It is a paid app, but it is worth it.

35. Cuba Junky is a good source of information

A brilliant blog about the country and excellent source to find casas particulares. You can upload Cuba Junky's map with the casas particulares onto your Galileo app to locate them while in Cuba.

36. Stay current with Havana Good Time

Havana Good Time is an iPhone app based guide of Havana that's fairly current and contains much more than the regular tourist spots.

Other Stuff To Consider

37. Havana is not dangerous, but scams are common

Other than petty theft, violent crimes are not common there. What many people do, though, is "friend you" and tell you about an awesome party happening at a restaurant or café, or some other event somewhere else. They will take you there, sit down, chat and drink/eat, and make you pay for everything. Additionally, they will ask for money for the "recommendations" given during your "lovely chat." They also get a commission from the restaurant. Don't be afraid to say no to them.

Having said that, Cubans are generally friendly, so don't be afraid to chat openly with them, but be cautious about their intentions.

38. You can buy or trade

Due to the trade restrictions, Cubans don't have access to many items we do. When purchasing souvenirs, it is possible the seller might offer to trade something (a t-shirt, pants, school materials, old used phones, a bar of soap, snacks, or whatever you have available) for the souvenirs. Economically, they might get more out of selling your traded items, and you virtually paid nothing for your souvenirs.

This is not always the case, but it happens often. Don't forget to haggle if needed!

39. You can now bring Cuban products back to the U.S.

Americans can now import up to $400 worth of goods from Cuba, including up to $100 in tobacco and alcohol products. So, now there's no need to smuggle those Cuban cigars, as long as they are under the limit.

40. Learn Spanish

It will make your life easier there. At least learn a few basic words to communicate. Locals are also way friendlier with tourists who at least make an effort to communicate something in Spanish.

The country might be a hassle to travel, and there might be a lot of limiting bureaucracy you might not understand, but this is part of the Cuban experience. You must go through it to live the richness of its culture, and up to a certain extent, the hassles of their daily life.

Hopefully, these tips will help ease the pain of the hassles, but should you want to enjoy Cuba without any hassle, both G Adventures and Intrepid Travel offer excellent and affordable multi-day tours all over Cuba.

50 Interesting Facts about Cuba

1. The Republic of Cuba consists on the island of Cuba, Isla de la Juventud (Isle of Youth), and several minor archipelagos.

2. Cuba is often called El Caiman or El Cocodrilo (Spanish for alligator), which is what the island looks like from an aerial view.

3. By land mass, Cuba is the largest island in the Caribbean, covering an area of 42,426 square miles.

4. With more than 11 million inhabitants, Cuba is the Caribbean's second-most populous island, and 16th most populated island in the world.

5. Cuba's original inhabitants were American Indians: the Ciboney (who migrated from the mainland of South America), the Taíno (who arrived from arrived from Hispaniola sometime in the 3rd century A.D.), and the Guanajatabey (who were located in western Cuba when Europeans first arrived.)

6. Christopher Columbus landed on Cuba's northeastern coast on October 28, 1492 near what is now Bariay in the Holguin province. Columbus claimed the island for the new Kingdom of Spain.

7. The name Cuba is thought to be derived from the Taíno language, and may be translated either as 'where fertile land is abundant' (cubao) or 'great place' (coabana). Others believe that Christopher Columbus named Cuba for the town of Cuba in Portugal.

8. Diego Velázquez de Cuéllar founded the first Spanish settlement at Baracoa in 1511.

9. San Cristobal de la Habana, which later became Cuba's capital city of Havana, was founded in 1515. Havana is Cuba's most populated city.

10. As the island development as Spanish colony, the native population declined rapidly due to disease and harsh conditions during the next century.

11. Large numbers of African slaves were imported to work the coffee and sugar plantations, and Havana became the launching point for the annual treasure fleets bound for Spain from Mexico and Peru.

12. Cuba remained a Spanish colony until 1898, although five different U.S. presidents—Polk, Pierce, Buchanan, Grant, and McKinley—tried to buy the island of Cuba from Spain between 1845 and 1898.

13. President McKinley offered Spain $300 million to buy Cuba just before the United States invaded during the Spanish-American War of 1898,

14. Under the Treaty of Paris following Spain's defeat in the Spanish-American War, Cuba was granted its independence from Spain, but was controlled by the United States.

15. In January 1899, the U.S. military took control of Cuba as a "protectorate," ruling the island until 1902.

16. Following three-and-a-half years of U.S. military rule, Cuba gained formal independence from the U.S. on May 20, 1902, as the Republic of Cuba.

17. During the next 57 years, the United States continued a strong influence over Cuba as the country cycled through a string of governments often dominated by the military and/or corrupt politicians.

18. In 1959, Fidel Castro led a rebel army of communist revolutionaries to victory. Fidel's authoritarian rule of Cuba would continue for almost 50 years until February 2008 when he stepped down due to health complications.

19. In March 1960, U.S. President Eisenhower approved a CIA plan to arm and train a group of Cuban refugees to overthrow the Castro regime. The Bay of Pigs

Invasion took place on April 14, 1961. About 1,400 Cuban exiles disembarked at the Bay of Pigs, but failed in their attempt to overthrow Castro.

20. The Cuban Missile Crisis occurred in October 1962. By 1963, Cuba was moving towards a full-fledged Communist system modeled on the USSR.

21. In 1991, Cuba faced a severe economic downturn in the aftermath of the Soviet collapse, causing a withdrawal of Soviet subsidies worth $4-6 billion annually. This time is known in Cuba as the "Special Period".

22. When Fidel Castro announced his resignation as President of Cuba in 2008, his younger brother, Raúl Castro, was declared the new President. In his inauguration speech, Raúl promised that some of the restrictions on freedom in Cuba would be removed.

23. As a result of efforts begun in December 2014 by President Barack Obama to re-establish diplomatic relations with the Cuban government, the United States and Cuba reopened embassies in their respective countries on 20 July 2015.

24. While the embargo between the United States and Cuba has not been yet lifted, it has been relaxed to allow import, export, and certain commerce within a limit between the two countries.

25. Meanwhile, the Republic of Cuba is one of the world's last remaining socialist countries following the Marxist-Leninist ideology. The First Secretary of the Communist Party is concurrently the President and Premier of Cuba. Gen. Raul Castro Ruz is both chief of state and the head of Cuba's government since February, 24, 2008.

26. The President of Cuba serves for five years and there is no limit to the number of terms of office.

27. Cuba's national legislature, called the National Assembly of People's Power, has 609 members that serve five-year terms. The assembly meets twice a year; between sessions legislative power is held by the 31 member Council of Ministers. Candidates for the Assembly are approved by public referendum. Cuba's Communist Party is the only legal party, and officially sanctioned candidates run unopposed.

28. All Cuban citizens age 16 and older who have not been convicted of a criminal offense can vote. The last election was held Feb. 3, 2013 with the next one in 2018.

29. Raúl Castro, current Cuban President, has announced his resignation for 2018 at the end of his current 5-year term.

30. Cuba is divided into 15 provinces and one special municipality (Isla de la Juventud). The provinces are divided into municipalities.

31. Cuba has the highest doctor-to-population ratio in the world and has sent thousands of doctors to more than 40 countries around the world. Cuban physicians played a leading role in combating the Ebola virus epidemic in West Africa.

32. Cuba is renowned for its music. The main musical form is called son, which is a combination of upbeat rhythms with classical guitar.

33. Baseball is Cuba's most popular sport. Boxing is also an important sport in Cuba with the country producing a number of Olympic champions.

34. Cuba has nine sites on the UNESCO World Heritage list.

35. Bacardi rum was originally manufactured in Cuba. However, the brand moved to Puerto Rico after Fidel Castro's takeover. Havana Club is the current run of Cuba.

36. A drink of rum and coke and lime is called a "Cuba Libre" in Latin America except in Cuba. There, it's called a "mentirita," or "little lie."

37. In Cuba, it is mandatory for government vehicles to pick up hitchhikers.

38. In 2000, Fidel Castro erected a statue of John Lennon of The Beatles in John Lennon Park in Havana. Castro admired Lennon and believed he was a true music revolutionary.

39. Cigars are called puros or habanos in Cuba. One company makes all the premium brands for the country.

40. Cuba has a 99.8% literacy rate, which is one of the highest in the world.

41. Major seaports in Cuba include: Antilla, Cienfuegos, Guantanamo, Havana, Matanzas, Mariel, Nuevitas Bay and Santiago de Cuba

42. The U.S. Naval Base at Guantanamo Bay is leased to the United States. The lease can be terminated only via mutual agreement or US abandonment of the facility.

43. Both men and women in Cuba are required to serve two years of compulsory military service between 17 and 28 years of age.

44. The Cuban government owns and controls all broadcast media including four national television networks and six national radio networks. Private ownership of electronic media is prohibited.

45. In April, 2011 Cuban Communist Party leaders approved a plan for wide-ranging economic changes. Since then, the government has slowly implemented economic reforms, including allowing Cubans to buy electronic appliances and cell phones, stay in hotels, and buy and sell used cars. The government has cut

state sector jobs as part of the reform process, and it has opened up some retail services to "self-employment," leading to the rise of so-called "cuentapropistas" or entrepreneurs. Approximately 476,000 Cuban workers are currently registered as self-employed.

46. Until 2011, there was an import ban on cars in Cuba. Hence, many of the cars on the road are classic cars from the 50's.

47. As few as five percent of Cubans have open Internet access, and having an internet connection in your home in Cuba is practically non-existent. Only government officials, academics, doctors, engineers, or regime-approved journalists have Internet access at work.

48. Cuban cuisine is focused on plantains, black beans and rice (referred to as Moros y Cristianos or moros), ropa vieja (shredded beef), Cuban bread, pork with onions, and tropical fruits. Garlic, cumin, oregano, and bay leaves are the dominant spices.

49. Cuba's terrain is mostly flat with rugged hills and mountains in the southeast part of the country.

50. Cuba has a tropical climate with moderate trade winds. November to April is considered the dry season while May to October is the rainy season.

VACATIONS IN EASTERN CUBA

Santiago de Cuba, located between the Caribbean Sea and the Sierra Maestra mountain range, is the Eastern capital and home of the Cuban Son, which is the father of all Cuban rhythms of this century. It is the capital of the Santiago de Cuba Province in the eastern region of the island and the country's second largest metropolis. This city, rich in culture, tradition, and also in natural and architectural treasures, provides travelers with amazing experiences in their Cuba vacations. From hill-walking and mountaineering to historical and cultural tours, Santiago de Cuba is a destination that will not disappoint you.

For those who love nature and who enjoy mountain-climbing and hill-walking activities, Santiago de Cuba offers several points of interest like: the Sierra Maestra mountain range and Baconao Biosphere Reserve, where La Gran Piedra (The Great Stone) stands out.

The rugged topography of the Sierra Maestra, with elevations of up to 1,300 m above sea level, is unique in the island and famous for its landscapes of breathtaking beauty and unbelievable variety. Among these elevations are the three highest peaks of Cuba: the Pico Real del Turquino with 1,974 m, the Pico Cuba with 1,872 m and the Pico Suecia with 1,734 m above sea level. This scenery gives the visitor the feeling of being at the top of the island, and you can literally touch the clouds in the sky. It is an exclusive place where one can get the best view of the rivers, forests, mountains and valleys that surround the region. It's also considered as one of the most important well-preserved areas in Cuba, due to the great diversity of its flora and fauna. I highly recommend bringing your camera along to take some pictures of endemic flowers and animals of the zone. Bird watching is also a popular activity in this area.

Moreover the Sierra Maestra is an emblematic site where decisive moments of the Cuban Revolution took place. In an intricate zone of this territory explorers can find the Comandancia de la Plata, the First Front of the Rebel Army, a place with historical value.

If you are traveling with the whole family, Baconao Park will be an excellent choice in your itinerary. Located in the Sierra Maestra, the Baconao Park was inscribed on the UNESCO World Heritage Biosphere Reserve List in 1987, including three well defined biogeographic zones: the "Meseta de Santiago", the

"Sierra de la Gran Piedra" and the "Meseta Santa Maria de Loreto". It incorporates beaches, mountains, lakes, forests and ruins of French coffee plantations. Visitors can appreciate a high biodiversity in flora and fauna, being a wonderful experience for nature lovers. Moreover, there is an International Diving Center and the Land Transport Museum, which exhibits over 2,000 miniature vehicles along with an exposition of vintage cars. Also, one can enjoy a visit to the Aquarium where dolphins and seals put an excellent show for both children and adults, exhibiting their abilities.

One of the main attractions of this zone is La Gran Piedra (The Great Stone), a majestic and magnificent rock formation. This enormous rock of volcanic origin is on the top of a mountain at 1,125 meters. Due to its gorgeous sceneries, this place constitutes a natural viewpoint. It is said that in the clear nights the lights of Jamaica can be seen from there. It's also considered one of the largest rocks in the world.

Have children? Take them to the Prehistory Valley, an amazing collection of reproductions of dinosaurs and other prehistoric animals made of stone in almost their natural size. These fantastic creatures are disseminated on a wide valley surrounded by mountains, in the same places where the legendary animals should have lived. This valley is a great venue for photography. Kids will love it!

On the other hand, Santiago de Cuba is an artistic and cultural centre of great prominence in the history of Cuba. Visitors' have the chance to enjoy historical tours in the midst of marvelous natural landscapes. Characterized by a solid historical background and cultural traditions, this city offers a wonderful display of historic sites such as the Cathedral, the first one in Cuba (1522) and the Casagranda Hotel which can be found in the city centre: by the Céspedes Park. Santiago de Cuba is the home of Cuba's oldest palaces and museums, including the Casa de Diego Velázquez also located in the Céspedes Park area. This zone continues to be a large part of the city's social life and it is known as Céspedes Park in honor of Carlos Manuel de Céspedes, a national hero also called the Founding Father or Father of the Homeland.

Among other significant buildings situated in the heart of the city is the Nuestra Señora de Asunción Cathedral. The Tour of the Revolution Square is also recommended. Best explored by foot, on your own or with one of the many guided tours available, Santiago de Cuba also has numerous museums and art galleries. One of the most popular museums is the Cuartel Moncada, the yellow barracks whose exterior is marked with carefully re-opened bullet holes, remindings of the July day in 1953 when Fidel Castro and a group of rebels launched an assault. It treasures the rebels' weapons, bloodstained uniforms, photographs, letters, and other documents. There's also the Granjita Siboney Museum, which was the place of gathering for the attack of the Moncada garrison. It now shows memorabilia of the assault.

Santiago de Cuba was the homeland of many notorious Cubans as well. That's why travelers can find in this city numerous museums that were the birthplace of famed figures of the Cuban history. One can visit the Native House of José María Heredia, one of Cuba's greatest poets; the Native House of Antonio Maceo, a leader of the war of independence and the Native House of Frank País, a hero who fought against the dictatorship of the 1950's. Furthermore, there are other historical sights to see in Santiago de Cuba such as the Museum of Carnival, which aims to give an overview of the great tradition of carnival in Santiago. It's also interesting the Emilio Bacardi Museum, one of Cuba's first museums that keep a valuable collection covering the period between the Spanish conquest and the Wars of Independence (from Spain). Other remarkable sights are the Museum of Rum that exhibits all about the great beverage and the Museum "La Isabelica", which shows some history of the French settlements in the area and displays farming implements and archeological objects.

One more historic attraction is the Santa Ifigenia Cemetery. This large cemetery is a small city of the dead, populated by elaborate marble tombs including several spectacular mausoleums. One of these belongs to José Marti, National Hero and one Cuba's most lucid and visionary men of all times. This cemetery gathers tombs for such historic notables as Carlos Manuel de Céspedes, the "Father of the Homeland", and Emilio Bacardi, including graves from those who fought for revolution, like Frank País.

Another world heritage site: The San Pedro de la Roca del Morro Castle can be found on the outskirts of this historical city. This fortress is one of the most formidable defensive works constructed by the Spaniards in the island. It was inscribed on the UNESCO World Heritage List as "the most complete, best-preserved example of Spanish-American military architecture based on Italian and Renaissance design principles". From this fortification the visitor can see the whole bay of Santiago de Cuba where took place the famous naval battle in 1898 between US and Spanish troops. The fortress now houses the Museum of Piracy.

Santiago de Cuba is also a centre of great religious importance. Located about 20 km far from the city the Iglesia de Nuestra Señora de la Caridad (Virgen de la Caridad del Cobre Sanctuary) is the most important shrine in the island. The walls of the church are laden with gifts from people that were healed or asked for the Virgin's blessing. Many are the visitors who come to Santiago to climb the hill of this sanctuary dedicated to the Patron Saint of Cuba. Some of them come to keep a promise, others take offerings which are added to the hundreds of pieces and objects that have been dedicated to the Virgin among which, is Hemingway's Nobel Prize medal. Some people often collect copper stones from the mine close to the church.

Finally, a journey to Santiago de Cuba would not be complete without sampling its cultural activities. Santiago de Cuba is famous for its celebrations, including the Festival of Caribbean Culture sometimes known as the Feast of Fire, and the popular Santiago Carnival which takes place every July. With the many festivals it holds, the city is called the cultural capital of the Caribbean.

Even though July in Santiago de Cuba tends to be extremely hot, it's probably the best time to enjoy its famous festivities. When the carnival begins in Santiago the whole city turns into one big party. What most characterize the carnival are the congas, which can be heard in areas such as Trocha or on any street. Contagious drum rhythms draw local people and visitors alike into one long flowing dance. Popular orchestras make their way to Santiago for the festivities. For the locals: music to dance to and plenty of beer is enough to make the carnival a success.

For those who appreciate other cultural pursuits and those who favor music and nightlife, Santiago de Cuba has its share of things to offer. Many music and dance venues exist such as the Casa del Caribe where tourists go for authentic Afro-Cuban shows and lessons; but Tropicana Santiago deserves a required visit. It is called the Cabaret of the Caribbean and it is considered one of the largest nightclubs in Cuba. The fame of Tropicana Santiago's shows has gone beyond Cuban borders, thus is a popular place if you are seeking night-time entertainment. However, there are other trendy places like the Trova House, a bar club where visitors can enjoy Cuban and Santiago's traditional music. Furthermore, the Heredia Street, very famous for its intense cultural and social life, leads visitors to better discovery of the best exponents of "son", bolero and a unique movement of troubadours.

CUBA BOARD GAME REVIEW

Rum, banks, hotels and a golf course or two. Now that's the life! You get to control all that and other facets of business and government in pre-revolution Cuba. Use your workers, architects, tradeswomen and mayors to develop and operate various businesses in this tropical paradise. Harvest products, ship off goods, cater to tourists and control government statutes to defeat the competition and become the most powerful person in Cuba!

Cuba is a strategy board game similar in both mechanics and theme to Puerto Rico and Endeavor. The game takes place in pre-revolution Cuba, and your goal is to become the most influential person on the island. Starting with your original plot of land full of resources and crops, you will need to decide how you want to grow your business to maximize profits and gain the most influence in government.

You could focus on producing sugar and converting it to rum and then shipping it off. You could even focus on raw produce and ship them off instead. Not interested in physical supply chain? You could focus on building inns, hotels and golf courses. Or you can take control of the banks and the market and bribe your way to victory! There are many paths to victory in this game.

The gameplay in Cuba mainly revolves around 5 action types or roles that you can play. You start the game with a 4 x 3 plot of land. Each square on the land can produce a product or resource, which include sugar, citrus, water, brick and wood. You produce these items by using the Worker role or action. You place the Worker on any square of your land, and you activate all buildings and produce resources and crops on the squares that share a row or column with the square the Worker is on. So if you want to produce more citrus this turn, you would place the Worker on a square that shares a row or column with 2 citrus plots.

The next role you can use is the Architect, who allows you to erect buildings by paying their resource cost. There are 25 buildings in the game, most of which are unique and limited. These buildings produce a variety of effects, such as converting sugar to rum, converting finished goods to victory points or cash, or passively producing victory points or cash. There are also special buildings that control ship movements, veto edicts and increase your influence in government. Erecting the buildings require you to put the building tile on a plot square on your land, effectively reducing the amount of crops and resources your land can produce. Since there are a limited number of these buildings, your strategy will have to be fluid enough to change depending on what buildings your opponents erect. The Architect also allows you to directly gain victory points instead of erecting a building.

The Foreman role allows you to use the abilities of all buildings that are located on the row and column activated by your Worker. The Tradeswoman role allows you to buy and sell crops and goods in the market. This is where you can sell stuff for cash, or buy more goods to be shipped or converted into other goods. The market in this game is organic and depends on player actions. If a large amount of one good is being sold to the market, its buy and sell price becomes cheaper. The Tradeswoman also has an alternate ability of getting a free resource or crop.

The fifth and last role is the Mayor, which allows you to ship your products. There are 3 ships sitting at the docks, with one more on its way to Cuba. Each of these ships accepts 5 specific products. Shipping these products will give you victory points. Supplying products to the ship that has been sitting at port the longest will get you more victory points. The Mayor also has an alternate ability which allows you to gain cash.

The catch is that there are 5 roles, but you can only perform 4 of them each round. The order you play them is also important, as players play 1 role each in turn until everyone has played all 4. The 5 roles also have an influence value, with the Mayor possessing the most influence, and the Worker possessing the least. Players compare the 4th and final role they played that round, and the player who played the highest influence role becomes the new starting player.

The role card that wasn't played that round is also important, as it influences how many votes you get in parliament. Players combine the influence value of their unplayed card with any cash "incentives" they wish to add, and this total value becomes their final vote. The player with the highest vote gets to pass into effect 2 out of 4 statutes or edicts that are available every round. These includes edicts that allow you to spend cash or goods to gain victory points, as well as ones that reward you for being good at one facet of business. There are also statutes that slightly change some of the game rules. Controlling which statutes are passed is important, as they will reward one style of play much more than others, and you always want the right statutes active in order to boost your chances at victory. The game lasts for 6 rounds, after which the player with the most victory points wins the game.

Cuba takes some of the most interesting mechanics and rules from the best games out there, and combines them into a package that somehow works beautifully. The premise is very engaging as well. Who doesn't want to be in control of the rum factories, hotels, banks and the corrupt government of a tropical island paradise? It is like the hit Tropico computer game, but in board game form. It is also supported by a number of expansion sets that add new mechanics and keep the game fresh.

DRIVING CUBA WEST TO EAST

To travel towards the Cuban capital and the rest of the country, that is, to the east of Cuba, and always by the coast, after leaving Cayo Levisa, one should take the highway that leads to Havana by the north littoral, the prettiest of them all where monotony is almost nonexistent as the route crosses many small picturesque towns. Just a little before reaching the town of Bahia Honda we are already in a coastal segment different from the route fragments left behind.

No longer will you find cays, mangroves and low coast lines, but, instead, high coast lines, where mangroves do not grow and cays are no longer present. It is the second segment of the north coast which extends almost to Varadero. The route till Havana City is entertaining and pleasant, along the north coast line and by the blue waters of the Florida Straight, which is always visible.

When asking a Cuban for addresses the word "oriente" should be used carefully. In Cuba by "Oriente" many only refer only to the 5 most eastern provinces in the Island: Las Tunas, Holguín, Granma, Santiago de Cuba and Guantánamo, those that, in the ancient Cuban political - administrative division formed the ancient province of "Oriente". This is why in the common language it is best to ask for directions using the names of the provinces instead of the cardinal points.

In Havana City, you may stay at any of the multiple available Havana Hotels to visit any of the beach groups that surround the Capital. These are commonly known as the Playas del Oeste (Beaches of the west) and the Playas del Este (Beches of the east) or the Havana north littoral beaches, in reference to its hosting city or province.

The first are commonly rocky and narrow beaches, deep and next to the new hotels in Havana. These are not continuous but are formed by segments interrupted by the coastal rocky groups. They are bordered by the urbanization. In some of them, a marine atmosphere is breathed and it is common to see small boats in the rivers that cross them. That is the case of Playa Jaimanitas and, a bit further down, the beach of Baracoa. Other like the Viriato and Marianao beaches, not very well known, are small mainly used by the neighbors of the close-by urbanizations. These are not very popular and basically visited only by very small groups.

Very different is the case of the Playas del Este or North Littoral beaches. These form a continuous sandy space, with mainly low depth waters and where the rivers that there connect can be easily crossed. Best example is probably the Boca Ciega River or Justiz River, which can be crossed shore to shore with under the knee waters which originate a by-the-coast lagoon system.

The beaches in the area receive different names and ar all crossed by small rivers. West to east you can find the Cojimar Becah, crossed by the River of the same name and that gives origin, just before reaching the coast, to a deep canyon to reach the sea due to fact that in the north coast are found the heights knows as the Habana - Matanzas heights.

Unfortunately, this river is somewhat contaminated although plans exist for its purification. In this site is located the small town that carries the same name of the river and its beach, Cojímar, famous after being immortalized by the north American writer Ernest Hemingway in his novel "The Old Man and the Sea". Clearly a place to visit here is the museum of the Finca La Vijía, Hemingways farm house located just nearby in San Francisco de Paula.

Passing Cojímar, the route borders the shore, and can bee seen from the highway. The first beach you encounter is the Bacuranao Beach crossed by the river of the same name. As a curious detail, it should be mentioned that in both rivers small fortresses can be found which were built by the Spanish to protect the newly born City of Havana against the attacks of pirates and corsairs, like the attacks occurred in 1762 when the English, under the commands of naval Commanders Albemarle and Pocock when the City of Havana was occupied for a period of nine months

Next to Bacuranao is the beach called Playa Tarará with its small river forming a small entrance that resembles an estuary locally known as the Itabo. Next are the beaches of Santa María del Mar and Brisas del Mar, which are the best known of all. They are really one single and very large beach with two names.

These beaches are both protected to the south by the mentioned heights which obligues you take the highway of Via Blanca in order to be able to reach them. This highway communicates the City of Havana with the province of Matanzas, the "Athens of Cuba", a city located by the Bay of its same name. The beaches can only be reached by four intersections from the Via Blanca. The first is located by Playa Tarará, the second in Boca Ciega, the third by the Restauran Gato Verde on 462 nd street which descends to the sea in a step-like manner crossing a terrace system of marine origin, similar to the one found in G street in the Vedado District, where four of these formations are distinguished while reaching the Malecón Seawalk, and the fourth on 506 th street, at a point knows as "La Conchita".

It is a really beautiful view if you stop at any of the high points of the mentioned elevations, especially at about 100 mt after passing 462 nd street, nest to the viewpoint knows as Bellomonte. This can be done at any time of day, although the best time is definitely in the early hours and the late afternoon when all can be clearly observed and exceptional conditions are available to view the beach, its wave trains, the different blue shades of the sea, vegetation and the construction sites of Guanabo and neighbor sites.

All these beaches, as in the rest of Cuba, are public. They communicate with each other easily from Tarará to Guanabo and it is common to see people begin the day at one extreme and end at the other. Almost 10 km are covered by these beautiful beaches. It is quite common to see groups of people and youngsters walking by the beach at any time of day.

There are several spots where you can obtain the necessary to enjoy of the sunny day. As to lodging, there are several Cuba hotels from Tarará to Guanabo like Villa Tarará, Villa Armonia, Mirador del Mar Villa Los Pinos, Hotel Atlántico and Hotel Las Terrazas. The best know, but now under repair is the Hotel Arenal or Hotel Itabo built atop one of the lagoons formed by the River Boca Ciega or Itabo without altering its vegetation, something similar to what is found in La Moka, in the Sierra del Rosario Biosphere Reserve.

But if you wish to stay in Havana City, just a some 20 km away, numerous Cuba hotels are available. The trip back by car is pleasant because the route by the sea actually offers different views when using the highway in either its two directions.

REAL ESTATE IN CUBA

Cuba is a country in an island only 90 miles south of the United States, became a communist regime under totalitarian rule over fifty years ago. Expropriated personal, business , and Real Estate property from its citizens,foreign residents, and foreign countries like United Estates under absurd and unjustified pretenses and never paid a cent of its value to anyone. They only achieved failure, waste, and disruption of lives and wealth. Natural resources have been depleted and damage to the ecology and environment have rendered the value of land worthless for modern use and development. Commercial buildings of beautiful Spanish, French and U S architecture have been allowed to deteriorate for lack of maintenance all over the country.

Modern farming and commercial enterprises at par with the rest of the world in efficiency and productivity became a product of a system reflecting similar failures in countries taken by Russia after the second world war. Which set back their progress for years behind most civilized countries. Russia's failure in Cuba to make it a satellite played a role in its downfall as the leading communist state.

Cuba's refusal to compensate for expropriations from the Unites States and all other countries that had investments in Cuba forced the United States to impose an embargo on Cuba, as a result, all credits and trade agreements were suspended, all credits, deposits, and monetary accounts of Cuba in U S banks, were frozen. and trade stopped. between the two countries. Capital fled by every possible means until the Cuban revolutionary government learned ways to stop the flow of funds in convertible currency like US dollars which had free exchange and circulation at par with the Cuba currency (peso). But land and buildings could not leave the country nor could they be sold to take their monetary value out of the country because the revolutionary government took control of all banks, property records, and converted the (peso) currency to a new peso of lower value making worthless and illegal the old (peso) currency.

Since then, obviously all property may not belong to the revolutionary government but they have full and absolute control over it. In the future will this change? The answer is yes.

Cuba had a preferential supplier quota of sugar to the US that had been earned by Cuba's l support to the US during the war years when Cuba was ruled by democratic governments. That sugar preferential vendor quota to the US had been the agreement that made Cuba one of the best economically developed countries in the world and the second highest per capita income of the American continent. Cuba's preferential sugar cuota was taken away and given in parts to four other countries in Central and South Latin America.

Russian economy was unable to sustain Cuba because their methods of development, production and distribution were never followed by a Cuban population set in the capitalistic ways of its closest and profitable trading partner the U S .

Real Estate starts with land and its best and highest use. if you buy raw land ,and pay a market price you will not realize a profit when you sell it unless the economy around it improves, or unless you change its use to a productive purpose. Because in a communist country all property belongs to the state and every citizen is under control of the state or the government,there is no personal initiative, interest, and much less freedom to perform, and do the best a person can do to improve his or her life and that of its family. Therefore at the individual level in Cuba, Real Estate has no value. Since Cuba controls all property from raw land to improved Real Estate be it Industrial, Commercial, or public service facilities. The Cuban government owns everything, and manages every producing element that keeps the country operating. They do it mainly by use of the members of the armed forces who have gradually substituted the regular workforce members of the Cuban society. Like in most countries including the US soldiers are paid lower than civilians regardless of job performance.

In Cuba, every citizen has to serve in the military, in a country where private enterprise is not permitted and anyone caught operating a private business is arrested,prosecuted, and given a jail term, the average citizen has minimal choices in life .

School is free, but most of the curriculum is political indoctrination to eventually feed the workforce, which is the army, they claim a free public health system of high quality, but it is not true, they put through free school, many doctors who never get a supervised practice and are sent to poor countries to serve people but in essence they practice their specialty without responsible supervision. Cubans have few choices, the army, a social work profession like to be a militant observer of their family and friends,a doctor with no practice, engineers with no jobs or a mere survivor in a society without private enterprise.

. When an individual can not follow the mentioned few choices this person becomes what they call in socialist country terms an "Anti Social" it means that person under much tolerance works when they find something to do like repair a car or household item, deal in black market of consumer items, and steal from the government anything that an army friend will let go unnoticed. When we examine this reality it is understood why so many risk everything to get out of the country by any means. A raft floating out to the Florida keys or Mexico, by marriage to a foreigner, or becoming a citizen of another country like Spain because of somehow proven ancestry.

Real Estate in Cuba was started as a colony of Spain, the early settlers who had the interest to raise cattle, or farm tobacco choose an area of land where of course were no fences. To claim a parcel of land a person could take a stick and throw it as far as it could and then mark a circle all around and measure the land inside the circle this was called a Hato or Corral, and it was then registered as a parcel of Real Estate it was a rudimentary way of knowing who owned the land so the system lend itself to numerous claims, with no solution in sight. We have to credit the late college professor and PHD in Commercial Science, Mr. Paulino Urbieta who as his thesis at the University of Havana made Real Estate and many other items of valuable research back in the year 1940 to continue improving and keeping better public property and statistical records using the metric system of measurement . It was prior to that year when properties started to be registered more accurately and measured by agronomists. Registration was done by a Notary Public who contrary to the method in US a Notary Public in Cuba had to have the same university credits as a lawyer, in essence, being a Lawyer in Real Estate Guardian of property records.

When the communist revolution came to Cuba in 1959, the government used property records only to distribute property in any way they saw fit to their particular plans and uses. Therefore most property records in Cuba are in deplorable disarray.

Many Cuban exiled second and third generation attorneys and realtors have been able to bring out Cuban property registration records of land, buildings and prime Real Estate with the purpose of establishing claims to recover properties taken away from their original lawful owners by the now fifty year old communist government.

The fact that over fifty years have passed under communism in Cuba shows only an struggle in this continent between Capitalism and Communism, something that Europe has experienced and continues to have in a somehow cooler confrontation, and now being called Socialism. It is spreading all over Latin America and becoming a threat to peace, democracy, and a peaceful social order in the region, it affects a person's right to Real property which is the starting point of progress, and a better life.

When Cuba and US move towards improved relations and US interests change, Real Estate will continue to be a value that can only function if its owners have their rights to use, sell, and pass it on to heirs.

For years to come Cuban Real Estate will continue to be a property very difficult to determine who owns it since the Cuban government has leased it to foreign investors, hotels and light industries have been built on it and rights to use have been given to other countries, even enemy countries of the US. Eminent domain is most common and the only way to designate the use of Real Estate in Cuba.

The fact that Cuba is only 90 miles away an small island surrounded by water and now part of the global economy and a spring board for other countries with ambitions, to resources and political domination in Latin America, sooner or later the US government, its people and allies will have to confront not what eleven million cubans have done but what a few thousand who make up the Cuban now called socialist government have done with the Cuban people and are responsible for having taken Cuba back in time and progress to the point of having reduced it to the second poorest country in the continent.

The Cuban people live in housing below our "Marginal" description of condition,several families of ten or more share homes built for one family and several homes share only one bathroom people sleep in bunks one over the other in two or more levels under one roof. People can not move from a home to another much less buy it so everyone rents from the government. When a real need comes for a larger or smaller home the family head goes to the housing government office but there never is a vacancy, the country is behind housing needs by unknown thousands of units. So a lot of illegal and tolerated housing activity goes on the streets or mainly in the towns central park.

Example- a typical "Anti Social" citizen knows someone who needs a larger house so at the public park he passes the word and soon someone shows up with another house or apartment to trade, they make a verbal agreement and pay a commission to the third party finder, then they go to the government office and request permission to make the switch which they usually obtain, as a result, that is the typical everyday way that a Real Estate transaction can be made in Cuba. by citizens.

In a very limited number Spain citizens have leased prime land and built condominiums for seasonal occupancy by tourists where the Cuban government is always a 51 % owner. it is doubtful that in a change in Cuba that this investors will be able to establish any legal claims from a new government, be it communist or capitalist.

For the next several years Cuba Real Estate will remain one of the worst investments anyone can make. For second homes, retirement homes , investments in resorts or any other Real Estate investment.

There are countries where Realtors who are professionals certified international property specialists members of the National Association of Real Estate and of their State and local association can provide an investor, buyer or seller of Real Estate a wealth of advise to reach a worthwhile and safe investment.

Conclusion

For those who appreciate other cultural pursuits and those who favor music and nightlife, Santiago de Cuba has its share of things to offer. Many music and dance venues exist such as the Casa del Caribe where tourists go for authentic Afro-Cuban shows and lessons; but Tropicana Santiago deserves a required visit. It is called the Cabaret of the Caribbean and it is considered one of the largest nightclubs in Cuba. The fame of Tropicana Santiago's shows has gone beyond Cuban borders, thus is a popular place if you are seeking night-time entertainment. However, there are other trendy places like the Trova House, a bar club where visitors can enjoy Cuban and Santiago's traditional music. Furthermore, the Heredia Street, very famous for its intense cultural and social life, leads visitors to better discovery of the best exponents of "son", bolero and a unique movement of troubadours.

Picture Credits:

www.flickr.comphotosikermerodio
www.flickr.comphotosneiljs
www.flickr.comphotospedrosz
www.flickr.comphotospixelbuffer
www.flickr.comphotoszedzap

Made in the USA
San Bernardino, CA
04 June 2017